Scottish Borders

3 4144 0083 8423 8

F

Older Generation

D1638973

Jim Gatenby

BERNARD BABANI (publishing) LTD
The Grampians
Shepherds Bush Road
London W6 7NF
England

www.babanibooks.com

Please Note

Although every care has been taken with the production of this book to ensure that all information is correct at the time of writing and that any projects, designs, modifications and/or programs, etc., contained herewith, operate in a correct and safe manner and also that any components specified are normally available in Great Britain, the Publishers and Author do not accept responsibility in any way for the failure (including fault in design) of any project, design, modification or program to work correctly or to cause damage to any equipment that it may be connected to or used in conjunction with, or in respect of any other damage or injury that may be so caused, nor do the Publishers accept responsibility in any way for the failure to obtain specified components.

Notice is also given that if equipment that is still under warranty is modified in any way or used or connected with home-built equipment then that warranty may be void.

© 2011 BERNARD BABANI (publishing) LTD

First Published – March 2011

British Library Cataloguing in Publication Data:

A catalogue record for this book is available from the British Library

ISBN 978-0-85934-723-5

Cover Design by Gregor Arthur

Printed and bound in Great Britain for Bernard Babani (publishing) Ltd

Preface

This book has been written to help older people, including those who may feel they have missed out on computing, to join in the social networking phenomenon known as Facebook. The book is written in plain English by an experienced teacher and author who is also a member of the Older Generation.

Facebook is currently one of the most popular methods of communication between friends and families all over the world. Hundreds of millions of people of all ages use Facebook to share news, information and photographs. With Facebook you can make friends and join discussion groups with people who share your interests or have a similar background to yourself.

The book starts with an introduction to Facebook and all you need to begin using this Web site, free of charge. The sign-up process to create a new Facebook account is then described. Then you can check your e-mail contacts lists for people who may wish to become your Facebook *friends* — the people with whom you interact and share your latest news and information.

The next chapter shows how to build your Facebook profile giving personal details (if you wish), such as your family, education, career, likes and dislikes. You can add a photograph as your profile picture although this can be added or replaced later if you prefer. Also discussed are *privacy* settings, essential to control who can see your personal information.

Facebook is one of the world's most popular photo sharing Web sites and the various methods of copying photographs from a camera and uploading them to Facebook are discussed in detail.

Also discussed are many other important features such as common interest groups, using Facebook on mobile phones and the promotion of causes, businesses, etc., and future events.

This book is by the same author as the best-selling and highly acclaimed "Computing for the Older Generation" (BP601) and "Getting Started in Computing for the Older Generation" (BP717).

About the Author

Jim Gatenby trained as a Chartered Mechanical Engineer and initially worked at Rolls-Royce Ltd using computers in the analysis of jet engine performance. He obtained a Master of Philosophy degree in Mathematical Education by research at Loughborough University of Technology and taught mathematics and computing in school for many years before becoming a full-time author. His most recent teaching posts included Head of Computer Studies and Information Technology Coordinator. The author has written over thirty books in the field of educational computing, including many of the titles in the highly successful Older Generation series from Bernard Babani (publishing) Ltd.

Trademarks

Facebook is a trademark or registered trademark of Facebook, Inc., Microsoft, Windows, Windows 7, Windows Mail, Internet Explorer, Paint, Hotmail, MSN are either trademarks or registered trademarks of Microsoft Corporation. BT is a registered trademark of British Telecommunications plc.

Firefox is a trademark of the Mozilla Foundation. Farmville is a trademark or registered trademark of Zynga, Inc. Blackberry is a trademark or registered trademark of Research in Motion (RIM).

All other brand and product names used in this book are recognized as trademarks or registered trademarks of their respective companies.

Acknowledgements

As usual I would like to thank my wife Jill for her continued support during the preparation of this book. Also our son David for checking the technical content of the book and our son Richard for providing the photographs of wildlife and diving in Sharm El Sheikh. Finally I would like to thank Michael Babani for his encouragement and for making this project possible.

Contents

5

6

Photos on Facebook

7

More Facebook Features

8

Copying Photographs to Your Computer 103

A Glossary of Facebook Terms   115

Conventions Used in this Book

Words which appear on the screen in menus, etc., are shown in the text in bold, for example, **Print Preview**.

Technical terms for devices which may be unfamiliar to the reader are introduced in italics, for example, *wireless router.*

Certain words appear on the screen using the American spelling, such as **Disk Cleanup** for example. Where the text refers directly to an item displayed on the screen, the American spelling is used.

Mouse Operation

Throughout this book, the following terms are used to describe the operation of the mouse:

Click

A single press of the left-hand mouse button.

Double-click

Two presses of the left-hand mouse button, in rapid succession.

Right-click

A single press of the right-hand mouse button.

Drag and Drop

Keep the left-hand or right-hand button held down and move the mouse, before releasing the button to transfer a screen object to a new position.

Further Reading

If you enjoy reading this book and find it helpful, you may be interested in a companion book by the same author, **An Introduction to the Internet for the Older Generation (BP711)** from Bernard Babani (publishing) Ltd and available from all good bookshops.

Introducing Facebook

This chapter gives an overview of Facebook and what you can do with it; later chapters give step-by-step instructions showing you how to get started and how to use the main features.

What is Facebook?

Facebook is a Web site which allows anyone to create Web pages about themselves and these can be viewed on a computer anywhere in the world. All you need is a computer connected to the Internet, a Web browser such as Internet Explorer or Mozilla Firefox and a valid e-mail address. You also need to be at least 13 years of age. Once you've signed up for a Facebook account you can start exchanging information with people you have chosen to accept as Facebook friends. Facebook, together with competitors such as Twitter, MySpace and LinkedIn, are known as *social networking* Web sites. At the time of writing Facebook is thought to be the biggest of these services with over 500 million users around the world.

Signing up for a Facebook account is free — the company derives its income from advertisements. A sample Facebook page is shown below with the advertisements on the right.

Am I Too Old to Use Facebook?

The answer to this frequently asked question is "Certainly not!" In 2010 Facebook had at least one prolific user of over 100 years of age, a lady with nearly 5000 Facebook friends. Admittedly Facebook had its roots among university students in the USA, launched in 2004 by Harvard student Mark Zuckerberg, who went on to become the world's youngest billionaire. However, with the rapid growth of the Internet, this form of electronic communication between friends rapidly expanded beyond the universities into the wider world. Facebook is now widely used by people of all ages and diverse backgrounds and is even the subject of a major film "The Social Network".

Recent years have seen Facebook become popular with millions of older people. This is not surprising since older people often want to keep in touch with friends and family who have moved away; it may be difficult or impossible for older people to travel to see children or friends in person. Facebook allows you to keep in touch electronically by exchanging news, photographs and video clips for example.

It's Easier Than You Think

Unfortunately many older people are mistakenly put off using computers, thinking they are too difficult to use and the exclusive preserve of youngsters. This is quite wrong — Facebook is easy for anyone to use and you don't need to be a young computer wizard or "geek" to enjoy it. This book takes you step-by-step through the stages of setting up your new Facebook account and using the main features.

If you are new to computing and need some help with the basic skills you may be interested in some of my other books from Bernard Babani (publishing) Ltd. These include "Getting Started in Computing for the Older Generation — Windows 7 Edition" (ISBN 978-0-85934-717-4) and "An Introduction to the Internet for the Older Generation" (ISBN 978-0-85934-711-2).

What Can Facebook Be Used For?

Listed below are some of the many Facebook facilities:

- Creating an easily accessible network of contacts collectively known as **friends** and also including family, work colleagues or perhaps customers of a business.

- Other people may send a request to become your friend and you can accept or reject them. You can invite people to be your friend and remove existing friends.

- Providing an up-to-date personal *profile* which your friends can read at any time. This includes contact details such as address, telephone number and e-mail address which may change from time to time.

- The profile can include details of your education and career and this may allow friends and colleagues from your past to contact you. If you include your interests and hobbies, likes and dislikes you may become a member of a Facebook *group* of like-minded people.

- You can include as much or as little information as you like in your profile and this can be edited or deleted at any time. You can set *privacy limits* so that information can be viewed by everyone or restricted to friends only and perhaps also friends of friends.

- You can build up albums of photographs on your Facebook page, easily accessible to all your friends.

- Communication between friends may consist of text messages, online "chatting" and also photos, video clips and links to other Web sites.

- You can use Facebook to publicise future events or promote a business. A group of friends with a common interest can join in an online discussion or a campaign.

- Facebook provides access to third-party software (known as *applications* or *apps*) to do specific tasks such as editing photographs or playing games.

Everything You Need

The only requirements to start using Facebook are:

- A computer with an Internet connection.
- A Web browser such as Internet Explorer or Mozilla Firefox.
- A valid e-mail address such as:

  johnsmith@hotmail.co.uk.
- You must be at least 13 years of age.

The Computer

The work on Facebook in this book has been carried out using a PC-type computer running the Microsoft Windows 7 operating system, but any PC or Apple computer made in the last few years should be quite adequate.

If you've already got a modern desktop computer this should be fine; if you're thinking of buying a new machine, a *laptop* computer or its small relative the *netbook* will give you the freedom to use Facebook on the move. Laptops typically have a screen size of approximately 15 inches, (measured diagonally), while the netbook screen is usually about 10 inches.

The Web Browser

Most computers use the Microsoft Internet Explorer Web browser to display Web pages such as Facebook, but you might equally use another browser such as the very popular Mozilla Firefox, freely downloadable from **www.mozilla.com**.

Firefox 3.6
Free Download
Windows (3.6.12, English (British), 7.6MB)

The Internet Connection in the Home

Internet Service Providers such as BT or Virgin Media provide fast broadband services allowing you to quickly access Web pages such as those on Facebook. Typical services cost £5-£20 a month depending on the package chosen and may include a free *wireless router* to connect your computer(s) to the Internet.

Connecting to the Internet While Travelling

The Wireless Access Point

Many hotels, cafés and airports, etc., provide *WIFI hotspots* i.e. *wireless access points,* enabling you to connect a computer to the Internet. Modern laptops and netbooks have the necessary built-in wireless networking components. This enables you to view Web pages such as Facebook while on the move. You may also need a *password* from the provider of the access point (hotel, café, etc.,) and there may be a charge.

Mobile Broadband

An alternative connection for users on the move is to buy a *mobile broadband modem* in the form of a *dongle* which plugs into a slot in the laptop or netbook computer. This will allow you to connect to the Internet and use Facebook via one of the mobile phone networks such as 3 Mobile.

Mobile Phone

Facebook can be accessed from the latest powerful Smartphones, which are really small handheld computers. These include the latest 3G and 4G (Third and Fourth Generation) phones such as the Blackberry and the Apple iPhone, which can handle broadband Internet. This is discussed in more detail later.

Your E-mail Address

You can't join Facebook unless you have a genuine e-mail address. When you first enter your e-mail address during the sign-up process (discussed shortly), any addresses which look false, comic or suspicious are rejected. For security purposes a confirmation e-mail is sent to your e-mail address. You must respond to this e-mail before you can become a Facebook user. This is to ensure that only people with a genuine e-mail address can join Facebook.

Your e-mail address is used as your login name every time you sign in to Facebook. The list of contacts in your e-mail address book is used by Facebook to find people who may wish to become your friends. If you have more than one e-mail account you can use several address books or contacts lists as the initial source of your potential Facebook friends. For example, if you have, say, **Windows Live Hotmail** and **Yahoo!** e-mail accounts as shown below, you would select each account in turn, then enter your appropriate e-mail address and click **Find friends**. Your e-mail contacts lists are then checked and anyone with a Facebook account is sent an invitation to become your friend, which they can either accept or decline.

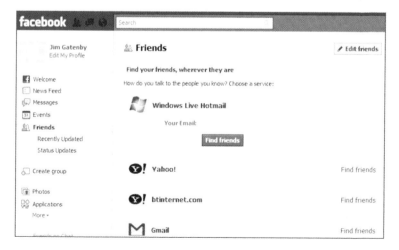

Creating a New E-mail Address

If you want to create a new e-mail address specifically to use with Facebook, Hotmail is a free and efficient service which is easy to set up and has hundreds of millions of users worldwide. Unlike some e-mail systems, Hotmail is a Web-based service, so you can use it easily from anywhere in the world, using any computer with an Internet connection.

Setting Up a Hotmail E-mail Account

Enter the following address into the Address Bar of a Web browser such as Internet Explorer:

http://login.live.com/

The following window appears from which you select the **Sign up** button as shown below. Signing up for a Windows Live ID also gives you access to other Microsoft services such as Windows Messenger as well as Hotmail.

Next, in response to the question **Do you have an e-mail address?** select **No, sign me up for a free MSN Hotmail e-mail address** as shown below. Then click **Continue**.

Signing Up to Hotmail

After clicking **Continue**, the **Mail** sign-up screen appears as shown below. Here you enter the first part of your chosen e-mail address to go before **@hotmail.com**. Click **Check Availability** to see if anyone else has already used the address. If so you can easily modify your preferred name by adding a number or perhaps your middle name or pet's name, for example.

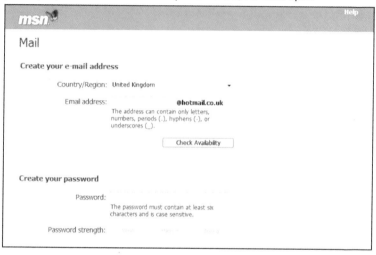

The rest of the sign-up process is quite straightforward. After choosing a secure password, you need to select a **Question** from a drop-down list, followed by your own **Secret answer**. You are also required to copy some distorted letters (known as a *CAPTCHA*), which appear on the screen. This is to check that a human being is completing the form and not an automated computer system which might be filling in the form for malicious or illegal purposes. Now finish the sign-up process by entering your name, gender, time zone and post code and accepting the terms of the Microsoft agreements.

With your new or existing e-mail address you are now ready to join Facebook, as discussed in Chapter 2.

2

Getting Started

Launching Facebook

Open your Web browser such as Internet Explorer and enter the Facebook address into the Address Bar at the top of the screen, as shown in the extract below.

(In practice you only need to enter **facebook.com** and the browser will add the **http://www.** part of the address).

Signing Up

The Facebook sign-up page opens as shown below. Enter your first and last names, e-mail address and a new password in the boxes shown on the right below. Then select your gender and date of birth from the drop-down menus. The date of birth is used to check you're at least 13 years of age. Later on your date of birth can be omitted from your profile page if you prefer that other people don't see it.

Existing users of Facebook also use the sign-up page every time they log in by entering their e-mail address and password as shown below and on the sign-up screen on the previous page.

At the bottom right of the sign-up page is a link (shown below) allowing you to create a Facebook page to promote a celebrity, band or business. There is also an option to create a community page to gather support for a cause or topic close to your heart.

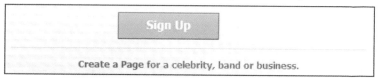

These alternative uses of Facebook are discussed later in this book; this chapter now continues with the signing-up process for the general Facebook individual user. From the initial sign-up screen shown on page 9, click **Sign Up** as shown above and you are presented with a CAPTCHA security check as shown below. Here you are required to type the distorted words into the boxes below. This is to prove that a human being is completing the sign-up form and not a rogue automated computer system being used for some clandestine or fraudulent activity.

After you click **Sign Up** the next screen gives you the chance to search your e-mail address book to see if any of your contacts are already on Facebook; then, if you wish, you can invite some or all of them to become your Facebook friends.

Finding friends is covered in more detail shortly, so for the time being click **Skip this step** to move on. The next step allows you to enter basic profile information, Secondary School, University and Employer. Here you can enter as much or as little information as you like. (You can add to or edit your profile at any time in the future.) Click **Skip** to move on or, if you have entered any of your profile information, click **Save & continue**.

The final step in signing up to Facebook allows you to add a **Profile picture**, as shown below.

This requires you to have a suitable photo stored on your hard disc or on some other medium such as CD or memory stick (also known as a flash drive or "dongle"). Or you can upload a photo directly to Facebook if you have a webcam attached to your computer. If you don't have a suitable photo to hand you can click **Skip** to move on. (A profile photo can easily be added later). Alternatively click **Save & continue** if you have added a photo to your profile. This leads to the completion of the sign-up process discussed on the next page.

Working With Photographs

Displaying photographs for others to see is an important aspect of Facebook. If you have photos on glossy paper they will need to be scanned and then saved on your hard disc or other storage medium. You can buy an inexpensive multi-function (MFP) inkjet or laser printer which has a built-in scanner.

Alternatively a webcam can now be bought for a few pounds and simply plugged into one of the small rectangular USB ports or sockets on the computer. Many new laptop computers are now supplied with a built-in webcam. If you are new to computing, these photographic topics are covered in detail later in this book.

Completing the Sign-Up Process

You should now find in your e-mail inbox a confirmation message from the Facebook team. This includes a link which you click to complete the sign-up process. Then the **Welcome to Facebook** screen appears as shown below. This allows you to start searching for friends, adding information to your profile, and activating your mobile phone to use Facebook .

At this stage you are now a member of Facebook and can start searching for more people to add as friends and if necessary expand your profile information, including adding a photograph.

Finding Friends

If you click the **Find friends** button shown on the previous page you are then required to enter the password for your selected e-mail account with a service such as Hotmail, AOL, etc.

When you click **Sign in** shown above, Facebook searches the list of contacts in your e-mail address book and produces a list of those who are members of Facebook. You then select with a tick those contacts that you want to be your friends, as shown below. Next click the **Send invitations** button and wait for your contacts to accept your offer.

Searching Other E-mail Accounts

If you have more than one e-mail account you can search all of your address books for potential friends. Select **Find friends** and a list of popular e-mail services is displayed. In the example below, **btinternet.com** has been selected.

Now enter your e-mail address for that service and click **Find friends** before signing into the service, in this case **btinternet.com**, with your user name and password. The list of your contacts with this e-mail service who are members of Facebook will be displayed, similar to the list at the bottom of page 14. You can then send invitations to any of these contacts who you wish to be your Facebook friends, as previously described.

Logging In to Facebook

You are now a member of Facebook and can log in whenever you want to using your e-mail address and password on the Facebook Welcome page as described on pages 9 and 10. As discussed earlier, this page can be opened by typing the address **www.facebook.com** into the Address Bar of your Web browser.

Creating a Desktop Icon for Facebook

With the Welcome page open, right-click anywhere over the page. From the menu which pops up select **Create Shortcut**. Then click **Yes** when you are asked if you want to place a shortcut to the Web site on your Windows Desktop. The icon is placed on your Windows Desktop. In future, to open the Facebook Welcome page quickly whenever you like, simply double-click the Desktop icon as shown on the right.

Creating Your Own Web Address for Facebook

With your own unique Facebook Web address or URL (Uniform Resource Locator) your friends, etc., can connect more easily to your Profile page on Facebook. They simply enter your URL into the Address Bar of their Web browser, as shown in the example for Samuel Johnson at the bottom of the page.

To create your own URL, enter **http://www.facebook.com/ username** into the Address Bar of your Web browser. For security purposes you must enter your mobile phone number. Then a confirmation code will be sent by SMS text message to the phone. Enter the confirmation code and click **Confirm**.

Then either accept the username suggested by Facebook or enter one of your own and click **Check Availability**. If your chosen name has already been used you will need to modify it, e.g. by adding a digit (0-9). Click **Confirm** to create your unique URL similar to the one shown in the example below.

Building Your Profile

Introduction

This chapter looks at the task of entering your profile information. You can enter as much or as little as you like but you need to be careful. Facebook has privacy controls which allow you to limit the information which certain categories of Facebook user can view. These categories are friends, friends of friends and everyone. If you enter lots of your personal (and possibly sensitive) information without setting the privacy controls, some of it may be visible to everyone. If in doubt, it's probably a good idea not to enter any sensitive information until you are familiar with the privacy controls, discussed later in this book.

The Profile Forms

Sign in to Facebook as discussed in Chapter 2, then from the **News Feed** screen under **Home**, click **Edit My Profile** as shown on the right.

On the left of the **Edit Profile** screen a list of the various profile forms appears, as shown here on the right. These are discussed in the next few pages. Profile pictures and photographs are also discussed again later in a separate chapter.

The link **privacy settings** shown on the right enables you to control who sees what parts of your profile, as discussed shortly.

Basic Information

The first of the forms is shown below. You can leave some of the boxes blank if you wish. There is a drop-down menu on the right of the form allowing you to hide your birthday or the year of your birth. On completing the form click the **Save Changes** button at the bottom of the form.

Adding a Profile Picture

Facebook makes it easy to add a photograph of yourself to your profile. If friends do a search for you they may find a long list of people with the same name as you. The photograph will enable them to select your correct Facebook page. You can add a Profile picture during the initial building of your profile or leave it blank and add (or remove) one later after clicking **Edit Profile** or **Edit My Profile** in the Welcome screen shown below on the left.

Uploading a Photo From Your Computer

As shown above on the right, there are two ways to insert a photograph into your profile. *Uploading* means transferring a photo from your computer to the Facebook Web *server* computer on the Internet. To use **Upload a photo** you must already have the photo stored on your hard disc or on some other storage medium, such as a *flash drive* (also known as a *memory stick*). You can also upload a photo to Facebook by connecting to your computer a *digital camera* containing the photograph. This can be done using a cable between the camera and one of the small rectangular *USB ports* (connecting sockets) on the computer. Alternatively take the *memory card* out of the camera and place it in an inexpensive *card reader*. The card reader has a cable to connect it to one of the USB ports on the computer.

If you need to use an existing photograph printed on paper, this will need to be *scanned* and saved on your hard disc, as discussed later in Chapter 8,

Click **Upload a photo** as shown on the previous page and the following window appears, allowing you to **Browse...**, i.e. search, your hard disc and other storage devices, for the required photo.

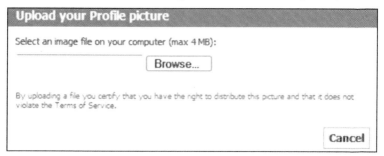

In this particular example, the required photo, **Stella and boys.jpg** had been scanned and was stored in a folder called **Family photos** on the hard disc drive **(C:)**, as shown below.

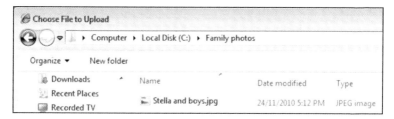

Click the required file name in the window as shown above and then click the **Open** button at the bottom of the window. You then have to wait a short time while the picture is uploaded to your Facebook Web page on the Internet.

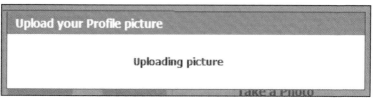

After a few seconds, the photograph appears as Stella's **Profile picture** on her Facebook **Welcome** page as shown below.

Taking a Photo With a Webcam

If you want to use an up-to-date photograph for your **Profile picture**, this can easily be achieved using a *webcam*. This is a small camera which can take photos and send them straight to the Internet. Many new laptop computers have a webcam built in to the top of the screen; for a desktop computer you can buy a separate webcam for a few pounds. This has a cable which plugs into one of the USB ports on the computer. It's simply a case of "plug and play" — after a few seconds the camera is ready to use.

When you click **Take a Photo** as shown above, the word **Loading** appears followed by a small box in which you click a button to allow Facebook to access your camera and microphone and then click **Close**. Now click the camera icon on the **Take a Profile picture** window shown on the right and then click **Save picture**. The picture appears on your Facebook pages as shown on the next page.

The Thumbnail Version of Your Profile Photo

A thumbnail is a miniature version of a photograph. For example, when you use the Facebook Search bar to find a person from their name, there may be a long list of people found with the same name. If they have uploaded a profile photo and edited their thumbnail, the thumbnail will appear next to their name, enabling the correct person to be selected from the list. From your **Home** page, select **Edit My Profile** and then click **Profile picture** on the left-hand side of the screen.

The **Edit thumbnail** window opens as shown below, allowing you to adjust the position of your photo by dragging with the left-hand mouse button held down.

Then click the **Save** button shown above. The thumbnail image is displayed around the Facebook site, helping other people to identify you.

Featured People

Select **Featured People** from the left-hand side of the screen as shown below, displayed after clicking **Edit Profile** or **Edit My Profile** as discussed earlier. In this form you can state whether you are married, single, in a relationship, etc., by selecting from the drop-down menu next to **Relationship Status**. You can also add family members and include their relationship (son, daughter, mother, father, etc.,) by selecting from the drop-down menu next to **Select Relation**.

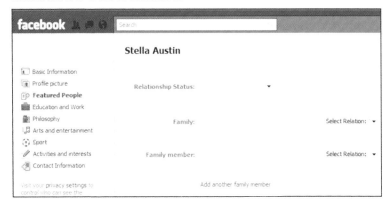

If you want to include further relatives click **Add another family member**, shown above. This produces further blank boxes under **Family** as shown below.

After you have entered all your family members, etc., click the **Save Changes** button. Note also that a relation can be deleted from your Facebook page using the **Remove** button shown on the right above.

Education and Work

This form allows you to enter your employment details, the schools you attended and any universities. Initially there are only single bars for you to enter your employer, school or university. After you enter an employer the form expands as shown below so that you can add further details such as your position, location and how long you have worked with the company, etc.

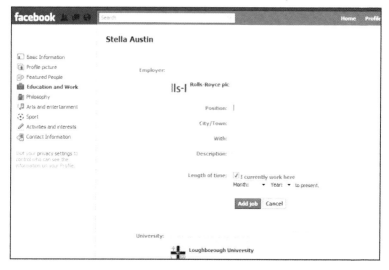

You can add further employers, schools and universities using the blue buttons such as **Add job**, **Add school**, etc.

As with the previous forms, you can leave boxes blank if you prefer. However, by giving details of your education and employment, Facebook can help you renew friendships with former school and college friends and work colleagues.

As discussed shortly, the privacy settings allow you to select who can view your information — friends only, friends of friends and everyone. Your Facebook pages can be found by anyone entering your name into the Facebook Search bar, so you need to be careful if you allow everyone to view your details.

Philosophy

Continuing with the list of profile forms, the **Philosophy** form can be opened from the menu on the left of the screen and shown here on the right. On this form you can if you wish, enter your religion, including a description. There are similar spaces for your political views, people who inspire you and your favourite quotations. As mentioned previously, you can, if you wish, leave sections blank. (You can always edit your profile at a later stage if you want to).

Arts and Entertainment

Here you can enter your favourite music, films, books, games and television programmes, etc.

Sport

If you're interested in sport you can enter any games that you play, teams that you support and your favourite athletes.

Activities and Interests

This section can include any of the (legal) hobbies and things you like doing, such as sky diving, gardening, cooking, photography, etc.

WARNING!

The personal information above helps Facebook to put you in touch with like-minded people. However, depending on your privacy settings, (discussed shortly), people who you do not know and may not be able to trust may also be able to see your interests and opinions.

Contact Information

This screen keeps your friends up-to-date with your latest e-mail address, Web site, phone numbers and home address.

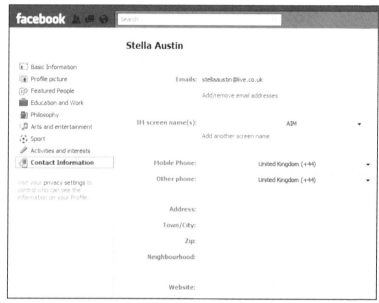

If you use instant messaging (**IM** above) services, enter your name as it appears on the screen. Instant messaging allows you to communicate with other people using real-time text messages. The drop-down menu displayed by clicking the arrow-head to the right of **AIM** shown above, displays a list of IM services. Select your own IM service, if you have one. You can also click **Add another screen name**, then add another name and also select another IM service.

Privacy Settings

The **Edit My Profile** feature on Facebook allows you to enter a great deal of personal information. It's possible for strangers to find your Facebook pages, using the Search facility, discussed shortly. Clearly there may be many details of your profile which you wouldn't want some people to see. Facebook allows you to tailor the privacy settings to control who sees what parts of your profile. Click **Account** on the blue Facebook bar and then select **Privacy Settings**. Alternatively on any of the **Edit Profile** pages just discussed, click the **privacy settings** link, which appears on the screenshot on the previous page under **Contact Information**.

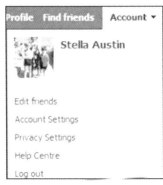

When you first create your profile, Facebook applies a **Recommended** set of privacy controls as shown below. Later you can edit these settings as you require. As discussed shortly, individual pieces of information can be set to be viewable by **Everyone**, **Friends only** and **Friends of friends**.

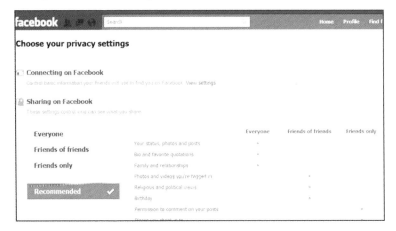

Changing Your Privacy Settings

Recommended

With the **Recommended** settings shown on the previous page and below, people who are not your friends can see some of your basic information. This includes your family, your work, education and things you

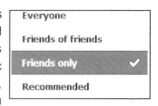

like. They will also be able to see your Facebook Wall. The Wall is discussed shortly but is basically a page listing recent changes you have made to your profile and posts or updates of your recent activity. People who are not your friends will not see your contact information, date of birth or political views.

Friends only

This will prevent people who are not your friends seeing some of your information such as the Wall, your family and your favourite quotations. With **Friends only** selected, people who are not your friends will only see your profile picture and list of friends. Selecting **Friends of friends** may make your personal information available to people you don't know personally.

Everyone

Selecting the **Everyone** privacy setting will make all of your information viewable by anyone who can find you on Facebook.

 When you've selected one of the four settings described above, click **Apply these settings** shown below.

Customising Individual Privacy Settings

You can tailor the privacy settings on individual pieces of information, such as **Posts by me**, **Family** and **Relationships** shown below. Click **Customise settings**, as shown at the bottom of the previous page.

As shown in the extract below, a complete list of all the pieces of information is displayed. Against each piece of information such as **Family** is a drop-down menu allowing you to make it viewable by **Friends only**, **Friends of friends** or **Everyone**.

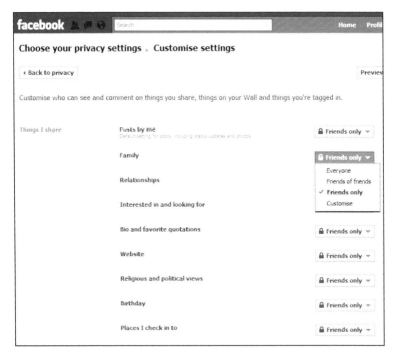

Customise shown on the right above allows you to make the information available to or hidden from, specific people Including named individuals as shown at the top of the next page.

After each individual privacy setting click **Save setting** as shown above. When you've completed your individual settings, an extra group privacy setting called **Custom** is added to the list of default group settings, i.e. **Everyone**, **Friends of friends**, **Friends only**, **Recommended** plus **Custom** as shown below.

When you've completed your privacy settings, click **Preview my Profile**, shown on the right of the top screenshot on the next page, to see how your profile will look to most people on Facebook. There is also an option to preview how much of your profile will be available to a specific person, by typing their name in the box containing **Start typing a friend's name**.

Who Can See What?

On the **Customise settings** page shown on page 29 there's a link **Preview my Profile** shown below on the right.

This opens a screen showing what information will be seen by most people on Facebook, with your current privacy settings.

Security Notes

- **Use the privacy settings to control who can see what parts of your personal information**

- **Do not accept as friends, people you don't know.**

- **Don't put information on Facebook that you wouldn't display on a notice board in public.**

Other People Finding You on Facebook

You can control the way other people find your pages on Facebook. From the top of the privacy settings page shown in the middle of page 30, select **View settings** as shown below.

Facebook recommends that these settings are set to Everyone to make it easy for friends and family to find you on Facebook. Also by allowing other people to send you messages and friend requests and to see your location, work and education, etc., you can make friends with people having similar interests. As discussed in Chapter 4, you can, if necessary, block people as friends and prevent them from communicating with you.

The Facebook Help Centre

For help on any aspect of Facebook click **Account**, then **Help Centre**, shown below on the right.

For further help on privacy controls, select **Privacy** from the list of help topics shown above. Click any of the text links shown below to get help on Facebook privacy topics, including **Take a tour to learn how to manage who can see your information on and off Facebook**, shown below under **Simpler privacy controls**.

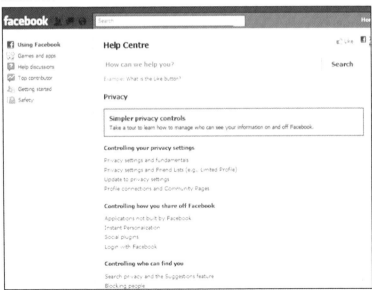

Your Facebook Profile Information in Brief

- Your Facebook profile allows you to enter personal information such as a photograph, your gender, date of birth, details of your family, education, employment, hobbies, interests and contact details.

- You can start building your profile during the initial sign-up process but it can be expanded and edited at any time in the future using the **Edit Profile** or **Edit My Profile** links.

- Your profile picture can be added to Facebook by uploading an image stored on your hard disc drive or directly from a webcam attached to your computer.

- A thumbnail, i.e. miniature version of your photograph, can be displayed on various pages on the Facebook site. This helps friends to recognise you and to be sure they are dealing with the pages of the right person.

- The information on your profile can be used to put you in touch with people who you may wish to invite to be your Facebook friends. These may be people you knew at school, college, in employment or who share your hobbies or interests, etc.

- Privacy settings can be used to control who can see your information; otherwise people you do not know may find you on Facebook and view important confidential information, such as your contact details.

- Blanket settings are available to restrict viewing to **Friends only** and **Friends of friends** or you can allow **Everyone** to access your information. There is also a **Recommended** group of privacy settings; alternatively use **Customise** to tailor the privacy settings on individual items of information such as birthday, family, relationships and contact details.

4

Finding Friends

Facebook Friends

The term *friends* on Facebook covers all the people you communicate with; this includes close personal friends in the "real" world as well as members of your family and colleagues from work and perhaps your student days. You can invite people to be your friend and they can accept or reject the invitation. Similarly you will be invited by other people to be their friend.

There are various methods used by Facebook to help you find people who you might want as friends, such as:

- Facebook scans your e-mail contacts to find people who are already on Facebook and suggests them as friends.

- Your e-mail contacts who are not already members may be sent an invitation to join Facebook.

- From your profile information, Facebook suggests people having something in common with you, such as your home district, school, college or employer. You can also initiate a search to find people with similar profile information and interests.

- If you think that someone may be a member of Facebook, you can enter their name into the Search bar in Facebook. If their name is not too common you should be able to find their page quickly from the list of search results, especially if they have included a profile picture.

- You are advised that Facebook users should not invite strangers to be friends or accept an invitation to be the friend of someone they don't know.

Finding Friends From E-mail Contacts

Your e-mail address is used in Facebook as your log-in name; from this Facebook can scan your e-mail address book or contacts list and find any of your contacts who are members of Facebook. This enables Facebook to suggest people who may wish to be your friends. Any of your contacts who are not members may be sent an invitation to join Facebook. You can also initiate a search of your e-mail contacts after clicking **Find friends** from the blue menu bar across the top right of the Facebook screen.

Make sure your e-mail address appears in the slot labelled **Your Email** in the highlighted e-mail service such as **Windows Live Hotmail** above. Then click **Find friends**.

If you have accounts with more than one e-mail service, you can repeat the **Find friends** process after selecting another service such as **AOL** shown on the previous page. Then enter your e-mail address and password for that service.

After you click **Find friends**, the following window appears:

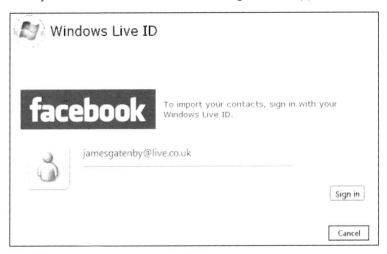

In the blank bar shown above enter the password for the selected e-mail service, not your Facebook password. After a few seconds anyone in the contacts list for that e-mail service who is a member of Facebook will be displayed; you can if you wish, click the small box next to the thumbnail picture and select **Add as Friends** if you want to send them an invitation.

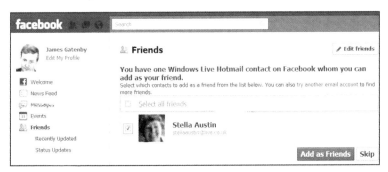

Accepting or Declining a Friend Request

When a user logs in to Facebook, they will see any requests to be their friend; they can then click either **Confirm** or **Not now**, to accept or decline the offer of friendship, as shown below.

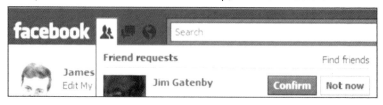

If a user clicks the **Not now** button shown above, they are asked if they know the person requesting their friendship. If they don't know them, they should click the **Don't know...** button. Facebook will then stop that person from sending them any more requests.

Using an Unlisted E-mail Service

If you use an e-mail service other than those listed on page 36, click **Other email service** near the bottom of the list. Then enter your e-mail address and password for that service and click **Find friends**. Any of your contacts on that e-mail service who are members of Facebook will be invited to be your friend. These contacts can then either accept or reject your friend request.

Further Searches For Facebook Friends

At the bottom of the list on page 36 there is a link entitled **Other tools**. Click this link and a list of searches is displayed, based on your Profile information.

 Other tools

Upload contact file

Find classmates from Bemrose School »

Find university friends, past or present »

Find former colleagues from Merrill College »

Upload contact file above means *importing* to Facebook a file of your e-mail contacts from an e-mail service which is not recognised by Facebook. First this file must be created.

Creating a Contact File for Uploading to Facebook

First you must create the file by *exporting* the list of contacts from your e-mail program. The file of e-mail contacts takes the form of a CSV (Comma Separated Variables) text file. The precise method for creating a CSV contacts file varies for different e-mail programs but the general method is as follows:

- Open the e-mail program.
- From the **File** menu select **Export**.
- Click **Accounts**.
- Click the name of the required e-mail account.
- Click the **Export** button.
- Select a folder on the hard disc drive to save the file.
- Give the file a name. If necessary select **.csv** as the file type.
- Click the **Save** button to place a copy of the file on your hard disc drive.

Uploading an E-mail Contacts File

As stated earlier, the contacts file only needs to be created if Facebook can't search your e-mail address book to find your contacts who are also members of Facebook. This may occur if your e-mail service uses an *e-mail client program* based on your hard disc rather than a Web-based system such as Hotmail.

Having created a CSV file of your e-mail contacts on your hard disc as previously described, it now has to be imported or uploaded to the Facebook Web site. Click **Find friends** from the blue bar across the top of the Facebook screen. Then under **Other tools**, select **Upload contact file**. Next click the **Browse** button to look for and select the contact file on your hard disc.

When you select **Upload contacts** shown above, Facebook lists those of your e-mail contacts who are members of Facebook and gives you the options to **Send invitations** or **Skip**.

Searching Using Profile Information

When you click **Other tools** as shown on the **Friends** window below, apart from the **Upload contact file** just discussed, Facebook displays a number of searches to find people you may have known in the past and who are members of Facebook.

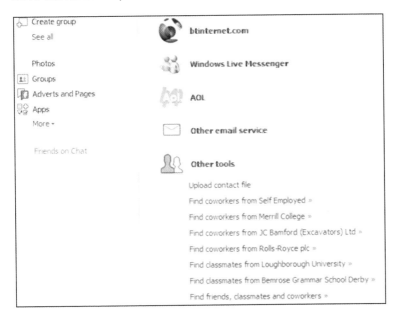

The searches are tailored to your own profile and designed to find Facebook members from your old school, college or employment, etc., as shown in the examples above starting with the word **Find**.

Clicking any of the **Find** options shown above produces a list of people whose backgrounds have something in common with yours. Any of the people listed whose thumbnails you recognise can, if you wish, be invited to be friends by clicking **Add as Friend**. Obviously a good profile picture enables you to be sure you know the person listed.

If you click **Find friends, classmates and co-workers** shown on the previous page, a list of people is displayed under the heading **Find friends from different parts of your life**. Depending on the amount of information you have entered in your profile, this may be an enormous list. This list is the sum total of all the people on Facebook who are connected to you in some way, based on all of your profile information, your friends and friends of friends.

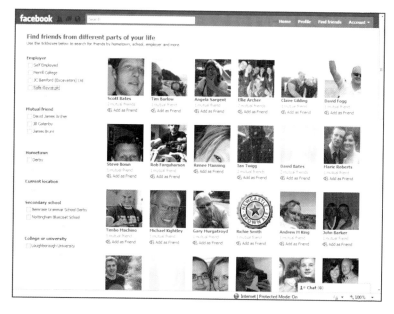

Tick boxes on the left of the screen allow you to filter out people from different parts of your life. Ticking more than one box will narrow down the search; for example, to find people who you were at school with and who now live in the same town, etc.

Searching for a Name

The Search Bar at the top of the Facebook Home Page allows you to enter the name of a person who may be a member of Facebook and who you may want to invite to be a friend.

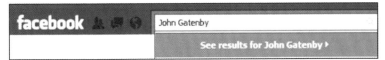

Click the link **See results for ...** shown above to display all of the people with that name or click the small magnifying glass. Unless the name is very unusual, you will find a long list of people with the required name. If they have included a recent profile picture you should be able to identify the correct record and click **Add as Friend** to send them an invitation.

If you're not able to recognise the person you want on the list, try clicking the names in blue. One of the records may display some information which confirms them as the person you're seeking.

You can also type the name of a personality, community, business or television programme. Many companies have Facebook pages giving useful information. For example, entering Rolls-Royce into the search bar produces several results giving information about the various Rolls-Royce companies including photographs, news and postings by Facebook users. Popular television programmes may have Facebook pages to which people have posted their opinions. These can include video clips enabling you to watch repeats of programmes on your computer.

Editing Friends

Once you've invited people to be your friend and they've accepted, you can list them by clicking the arrow next to **Account** to open the drop-down menu shown on the right. Then select **Edit Friends**.

From the drop-down menu under **Friends** shown in bold on the left below, select **All Friends** instead of **Recently Interacted**, which appears by default.

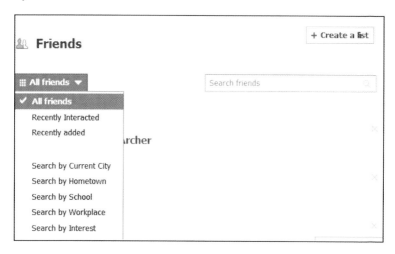

The complete list of your friends appears as shown on the next page. If you've made a lot of Facebook friends, this list will extend to many pages. Apart from listing **All friends**, you can also display **Recently added** friends and those with whom you have **Recently interacted** by exchanging messages, etc.

Removing a Friend

The crosses to the extreme right of each name above allow you to remove a friend if necessary. When you click the cross you are asked if you are sure you wish to remove the friend, as shown below.

Searching Amongst Friends

The menu on the previous page includes options to search amongst your friends on Facebook, for those who meet certain criteria. When you select a search such as **Search by School**, an appropriate blank search bar appears as shown below.

When you start typing the name of the school you may be given some suggestions from the first few letters. After the name of the school is entered any of your friends who attended are listed as shown below.

Creating a Friend List

After clicking **Create a list**, as shown above, you can click those people who you want to appear in the list. Lists can help you to set different privacy levels, as discussed on the next page and in the previous chapter, for particular groups of friends. In the example below a list called **Relations** has been created.

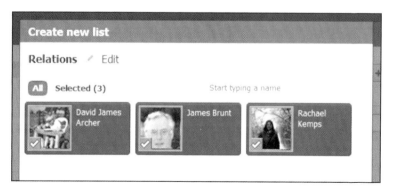

Privacy Settings and Friend Lists

Suppose you had created a friend list called **Relations**. You could use your privacy settings to make sure they alone could see a particular part of your profile such as **Family**. From the **Account** menu select **Privacy Settings** and then click **Customise settings** next to the pencil near the bottom of the privacy settings screen. Down the left of the **Customise settings** screen which appears are information headings such as **Posts by me**, **Family** and **Relationships** shown below.

To the right of each item of information above there is a drop-down menu allowing you to select who will be allowed to view the item, as shown for **Family** above. Click **Customise** at the bottom of the menu and the **Custom privacy** window appears, as shown below. From the drop-down menu to the right of **These people** select **Specific people...** as shown below. Then in the blank bar which appears type the name of the friend list (**Relations** in this example) which is to see the information.

Blocking Users

You can use the **Block** feature to prevent people from seeing your profile. You will not appear in their search results or in their friend lists. Blocking is *mutual*, so both you and the person you are blocking are affected in the same way.

From the **Account** menu on the blue bar across the top of the Facebook screen, select **Privacy Settings**. Then from the bottom of the privacy settings screen, under **Block lists**, click **Edit your lists** as shown below.

As shown below, you can enter the names of people who you no longer want as friends and stop them sending you invitations to future events or to interact with you in applications (programs such as games, etc.)

Using Facebook

Introduction

Earlier chapters looked at the setting up of a new Facebook account and the entry of information about yourself in your personal profile. The last chapter showed how to search your e-mail contacts lists for people who are members of Facebook and how they may confirm or ignore your request to become a Facebook friend. This chapter shows how you can start to use Facebook to communicate with friends.

Signing In

Open the Facebook sign-in page by entering the address **www.facebook.com** into the address bar of your Web browser or by double-clicking an icon on the Windows Desktop as described on pages 9 and 16. Then enter your e-mail address and password as shown below and click the **Log in** button.

Unless you are the only person who uses this particular computer, you may not wish to click to place a tick in the box next to **Keep me logged in**. If you do tick the box people who are not your friends may be able to read information which you'd rather not share with them.

After you click the **Log in** button, Facebook opens with your **Home** page displaying your **News Feed**, as shown on the next page. Your News Feed displays recent Facebook activity and exchanges of information between you and your friends. These exchanges are known as **status updates**.

The blue bar shown above is always present across the top of the Facebook screen; on the left of the bar the word **facebook** can be clicked to return to your **Home** page at any time.

To the right of the word **facebook** above there are three rather faint icons. These can be clicked to find out if there are any **Friend requests**, new **Messages** or **Notifications**. These are discussed elsewhere in this book. As discussed shortly, Messages are different from News Feeds. Messages are between you and one or more named contacts, similar to an e-mail. News Feeds can be viewed by friends, friends of friends or everyone, depending on your privacy settings, as discussed in Chapter 3.

Across the top right of the screen shown above are links to four main features of Facebook, namely **Home**, **Profile**, **Find friends** and **Account**.

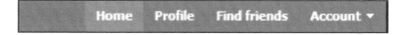

The Home page opens with the **News Feed** displayed as shown in the extract at the top of the next page. This shows any recent posts (also known as updates) from your friends and also status updates you've posted yourself.

The News Feed also displays the Facebook activities of your friends such as the fact that Stella has the new Facebook profile design (introduced in late 2010). Posts of this type about your Facebook activities are generated by Facebook itself.

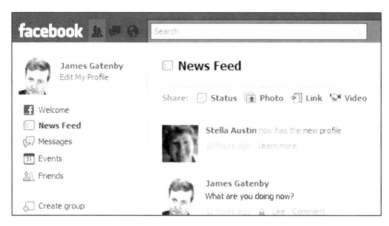

Wherever a person's name appears in blue on Facebook, a single click will display that person's profile as far as their privacy settings will allow. To return to your own Home page click the word **facebook** or the word **Home** on the blue bar.

On the left-hand side of the Home screen shown above, the link **Edit My Profile** allows you to make changes to your personal information such as employment details, likes and dislikes and address and telephone number.

The **Welcome** feature shown below enables you to add to your profile, set up your mobile phone for use with Facebook, find new Facebook friends and control how your information is shared, using the **privacy settings** option.

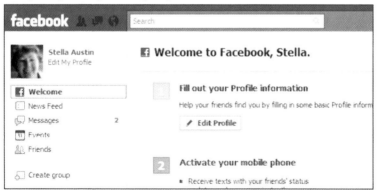

Posting a Status Update

This is the quickest and most popular method of communication between Facebook users. It's used for short messages telling friends what you are currently doing and thinking. With **News Feed** selected, as shown below, click the word **Status** near the middle of the screen. An empty box appears allowing you to enter a short statement in response to **What's on your mind?**

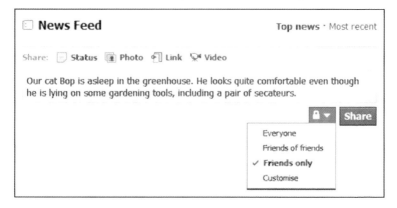

After entering the text of your message, as shown above, click the small arrow next to the padlock icon. Then select who you want to allow to be able to view the update. Choose from **Everyone**, **Friends of friends**, **Friends only** or **Customise**. Customise allows you to make the message visible to, or hidden from, specific people. then click **Share** button to send the update to your friends.

When Stella types an update about her cat, as shown on the previous page and clicks **Share**, the update appears immediately at the top of her News Feed, as shown below.

The update also appears on Stella's Facebook Wall, part of her Facebook Profile, discussed shortly. Depending on the privacy settings chosen, anyone who can view Stella's Wall will be able to see the status updates she has posted. Access to your Wall by a person who is not your friend can be prevented using your privacy settings, as discussed in Chapter 3, pages 27 onwards.

When Stella's friends, (such as James below), log on to their Facebook Home page they should immediately see the latest post about her cat near the top of their News Feed. James can leave a comment if desired and this will quickly be viewable on Stella's News Feed.

When you click the **Share** button the status update including the photo and text is posted to your News Feed and to your Wall as shown below. The Wall is part of your Facebook Profile and is discussed in more detail shortly.

Clicking the photo of the cat shown above enlarges it to fill most of the screen. James, as a friend of Stella, receives a similar update in his Home page under News Feed as shown below.

Posting a Web Link

If you think your friends may be interested in a particular Web site, you can send a live link as part of a status update. Click the word **Link** on the News Feed page or on your Wall and enter the address, for example, **www.babanibooks.com**.

When you click **Attach** as shown above, a blank bar is displayed for you to enter the text of your status update as shown below.

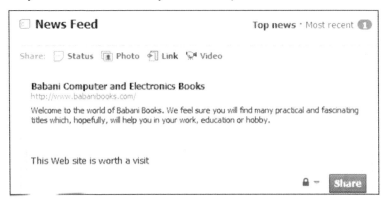

After you click **Share** the status update appears on your friends' News Feed together with the live Web link as shown below. Your friends only have to click the link to open the Web site.

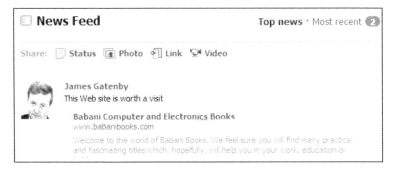

Posting a Video

To share a video with your friends you need to have it saved as a file on your computer, either on your hard disc or on some other storage medium such as a flash drive or CD/DVD. Alternatively you can record a new video using a webcam connected to your computer, as discussed elsewhere in this book. Click the **Video** link under **News Feed** as shown below. This link is also available on your Wall, part of your Profile.

Recording a Video Using a Webcam

If you click **Record a Video** and then **Allow** and **Close**, you are presented with a viewing window and buttons to start and stop the recording as shown on the right. After you stop recording, a small bar appears in which you can type a note about the video.

Uploading a Video

When you click **Upload a Video** shown on the right above, you can browse through the folders on your computer to find the required video file, as shown at the top of the next page. Please note that there is a limit of 100MB or 2 minutes on the size of the video. This information appears when you select **View** then **Details** in the Windows Explorer as shown below.

Videos library

Sample Videos

Name	Date	Type	Size	Length
Wildlife.wmv	14/07/2009 5:52 AM	Windows Media A...	25,631 KB	00:00:30

Sharing a Video

After you've recorded your video with a webcam or browsed for a video stored on your computer, you're ready to share it with your friends. As shown above, you can say something about the video before clicking the padlock icon to set the privacy such as **Friends only**, etc. When you click the **Share** button shown above, the video is posted to your News Feed, your Wall and to the News Feeds of your friends. A small image of the video appears together with a blue and white Play button to start the video, as shown below.

Messages

This feature is different from the status updates just described. Whereas an update is posted to your Wall and can be viewed by and commented on by anyone with sufficient access to view your Wall, a message is sent to one or more specific people, like an e-mail. Other people will not be able to see it.

Make sure you're on your Home page by clicking **Home** on the right-hand side of the Facebook screen or by clicking the word **facebook** on the blue bar as shown on the right. Select **Messages** from the menu on the left of the screen, and click the **+ New message** button shown below.

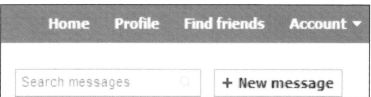

Then enter the name or e-mail address of a friend or the name of a Facebook list of friends as discussed in Chapter 4.

The **New message** window at the
bottom of the previous page has icons to
allow you to attach photos, videos or

Web links, as shown on the right. The method for attaching these
media is similar to that described on the previous pages for
including media with a status update.

When Stella has finished the message, clicking **Send** will place a
copy in the Message area of the recipient's Home page. Next
time the recipient, in this case James, signs in to Facebook they
can read the message and if necessary send a reply. An extract
from James' Message area is shown below. After entering the
text, James would click the **Reply** button to send it on its way.

The reply is sent to Stella's message area, where a number,
shown below to the right of **Messages**, indicates that there are
new messages. On clicking **Messages** shown below, the reply
from James is displayed on
Stella's screen. Messages can
be deleted after clicking a cross
on the extreme right of the
message.

Another Look at the Wall

The Wall keeps a record of all your recent activity on Facebook. It's part of your Profile which can be accessed from the blue bar across the top of the Facebook Home screen.

After you click **Profile** your Wall is displayed automatically. It can also be selected at other times by clicking **Wall** on the small menu shown on the left, which appears on the left-hand side of the Profile page. An extract from the Wall is shown below.

At the top of the Wall is some basic information about you and there are links to add to it or change it after clicking **Edit Profile**. Facebook displays up to five of your photographs near the top of the screen and there is the Status bar enabling you to post new messages on your Wall and on the Home pages of your friends under News Feed, as discussed earlier in this chapter. Simply enter the text of your update where it says **What's on your mind?**, as shown on the previous page. In the body of the Wall are the updates you have posted such as the one below containing the Web link **www.babanibooks.com**.

James Gatenby
This Web site is worth a visit

Babani Computer and Electronics Books
www.babanibooks.com

Your friends can view a copy of the update on their Home page under News Feed. They can also click **Like** to indicate their agreement or approval if appropriate and add a comment, which will appear on your Wall.

RECENT ACTIVITY near the bottom of the previous page shows a log (created by Facebook) of what you've been doing on Facebook. This includes changes to your profile, such as employment details, new Facebook friends you've accepted and comments you've made about other people's posts. Comments by other people on your posts may appear on your Wall if your privacy settings permit this. You can control access to your posts, etc., after selecting **Account** from the blue Facebook bar. Then click **Privacy Settings** and **Customise settings** and choose a setting such as **Friends only**, from the drop-down menu as shown below.

Writing on a Friend's Wall

You can post a message directly on a friend's Wall quite easily.
First sign into your own Facebook account.

Then find your friend's Facebook pages by entering their name
into the Search bar on the blue bar across the top of the
Facebook screen.

Select your friend from the list of people found in the search.
Alternatively select your friend from the list displayed after
clicking **Friend**. Your friend's Wall is displayed automatically as
shown below.

Now write the text of your message on your friend's Wall in the
bar shown above under **Post**, replacing **Write something...**.

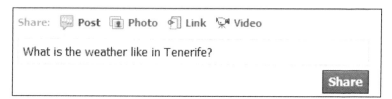

When you click **Share**, the message you've written appears as a new post at the top of your friend's Wall. It also appears on your friend's Home page under News Feed.

The message also appears on your own Home page under **News Feed** as shown below.

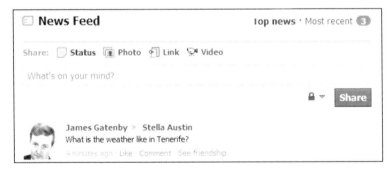

The message you have written on your friend's Wall does not appear on your own Wall.

A Facebook Case Study — Wildlife Rescue

We came across this site after a tawny owl flew into our car and appeared to be mortally wounded. We needed to find specialist help to save the owl's life. Fortunately a search using Google quickly led to the Facebook pages of the Burton Wildlife Rescue and Animal Centre shown below. With their care the owl made a complete recovery and was released back into its natural habitat.

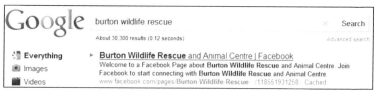

Clicking the above Web link opens the centre's **Info** page giving details of their history and their contact information.

At the time of writing many Facebook sites were still using the tabs such as **Wall**, **Info**, **Photos**, etc., shown above. As discussed elsewhere in this book, a new Profile design was introduced at the end of 2010. This replaced the tabs with links down the left-hand side of the screen to features such as the **Wall**, **Info**, **Photos** and **Events**.

A very worthwhile use of the Facebook Wall is shown below. The centre posts updates of their latest animal rescues and the public can respond by posting comments including offers of help, shown against a blue background in the example below.

Burton Wildlife Rescue and Animal Centre Rescued an owl yesterday, quite thin due to being stuck in a horse stable for 5 days. Also big operation by me (Lindsay), and volunteers Maz and Andrea to rescue a goose at dallow bridge stuck in the ice. Had to get boat to reach it on other side - took us an hour and a half to pick our way through the ice to get too it!!!

30 November at 17:51

👍 3 people like this.

💬 View all 7 comments

Elaine Ratcliffe Ok thanks Lyndsay,just wondered as we have a Barn owl ourselves, have you got food?

01 December at 10:29 · Flag

The Wall is also used to post progress reports on the recovery of sick animals; dogs and cats are found new homes as a result of posts on the Wall.

The **Events** feature shown as a tab on the previous page is used to publicise future fund-raising activities such as car boot sales. Facebook also allows extensive albums of photographs to be displayed, as discussed shortly in a separate chapter. The rescue centre uses this feature to allow prospective new owners to view animals that are available for rehoming.

Burton Wildlife Rescue and Animal Centre's Albums 5 Photo Albums

DOGS FOR REHOMING
3 photos

random
61 photos

REHOMED animals
6 photos

The Chat Feature

This allows you to communicate in real time with Facebook friends who are currently online. A small rectangle at the bottom right of the screen shows whether you have any friends currently online.

Click the rectangle to see who is online and then select anyone you want to chat to. The window shown on the right below appears. Type your first message at the flashing cursor in the bar at the bottom.

When you press **Enter** or **Return** the message should appear in your own chat window as shown on the right. It will also appear in your friend's Chat window. As the conversation continues your messages and those of your friend all appear in your respective windows as shown above on the right.

Clicking **Options** shown above allows a sound to be played when a new Chat message is received on your computer, as shown on the right. There is also a **Pop Out Chat** button to make the Chat window fill the whole screen.

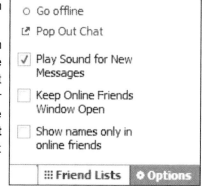

The Poke Feature

This is just a very simple way of saying hello and telling someone you're online on Facebook. The **Poke** button does not appear on your own Wall; it appears when you view a friend's Wall on your computer, as shown below.

When you click the Poke button above, you are given the chance to continue with the **Poke** or **Cancel**.

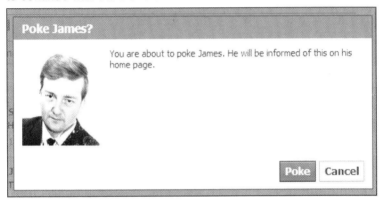

Your friend receives a notification of the Poke on their Home page. When you receive a poke from someone else, you are given the chance to poke them back.

As shown at the top of the page, when you view a friend's Wall there are buttons to take you straight to the **Chat** and **Send message** features discussed earlier. There is also an opportunity to suggest possible friends for the friend whose Wall you are currently viewing.

Some Important Features of Facebook

- The Info section of your Profile lists details of your education, employment, likes and dislikes and contact details.

- The Wall is part of your Profile and consists of Status Updates or Posts; these are short notes on the Wall telling your friends what you are doing or thinking and also listing any changes you've made to your Profile information.

- Updates can also include photos, videos and links to other Web sites.

- Updates appear as News Feeds on your friends' Home Pages, allowing them to read the text, view photos and videos and open links to other Web sites.

- Photos and videos can be uploaded to Facebook from your hard disc drive or some other storage location on your computer. Alternatively new photos and videos can be prepared using a webcam attached to your computer, before being shared with your friends as posts or updates.

- Other people may be able to write Comments on your updates or click the Like button to express agreement.

- Other people may be able to write updates on your Wall.

- You can use your Privacy Settings to control who can see your Wall, write messages on it and write comments on your posts.

- The Privacy Settings allow you to make your Facebook site and various operations accessible to Everyone, Friends of Friends, Friends Only or to specified people.

- The Messages feature in Facebook is different from a status update, since it is sent to (and only viewable by) one or more named people. The Facebook Message can include an attached photo, Web link or video clip.

Photos on Facebook

Introduction

Earlier chapters have shown how you can include a photograph as part of your Facebook profile. The thumbnail version of this is used around the Facebook site so that your friends know they are looking at your pages and not those of someone else with the same name as you.

This chapter shows how Facebook can be used as a photo-sharing Web site, enabling your friends and family worldwide to see your latest photographs. You might want to share images of your latest holiday or a major social event such as a wedding or party. If you have lots of photographs these can be arranged in numerous albums, each album containing up to 200 images. There are several ways of putting photos onto Facebook:

- Use a Webcam to take a current photograph and upload it directly to your Facebook Web page.

- Locate photos already saved on your computer's internal hard disc drive and upload them to the Facebook Web site on the Internet. Facebook makes this a very simple operation.

- Alternatively photos may be uploaded from another storage medium such as a CD, DVD or flash drive (also known as a memory stick).

Copying Photographs to Your Computer

This chapter assumes that you know how to transfer photos to your hard disc from a digital camera or by scanning a photographic print. If you need help with these topics please read Chapter 8, Copying Photographs to Your Computer.

Using a Webcam

Many new laptop computers have a built-in webcam, which takes the form of a small aperture set in the top of the laptop screen. If you have a desktop computer you can buy a separate webcam for just a few pounds. This usually has a long cable which plugs into one of the small rectangular USB ports on the front or back of the computer, as shown on the right. The cable allows you to move the camera about to photograph objects away from the computer. More freedom can be obtained by increasing the length of the webcam cable with a USB extension lead. This will allow you to take photographs outside in your garden, for example, as shown on the next page. Alternatively the separate webcam may be clipped to the top edge of the monitor as shown below, to take your Facebook profile photo, for example.

To start using the webcam, log in to Facebook and click **Photo** from the top of your Home page as shown below.

Now click **Take a Photo** and the photo window opens on the screen. Click the circular radio button next to **Allow**, as shown on the right and then click **Close**. Click the camera icon (shown below) at the bottom of the window to take the photo.

Sharing a Photograph

Now click the small arrow on the right of the padlock icon near the bottom of the screen and shown here on the right. This allows you to select the privacy for the photograph, such as **Friends only**. The **Customise option** shown on the right lets you

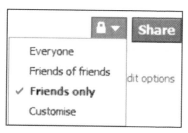

make the photograph viewable by, or hidden from, specified people. When you click **Share** shown above, a photograph is posted on your Wall and on your Home page under **News Feed**. It will also appear as a News Feed on your friends' Home pages.

When you click an image on the Wall or News Feed shown above, a large version appears with options to edit the photograph, as described at the bottom of page 84.

Viewing Other People's Photos on Their Wall

A photograph will be viewable by anyone who can see your Wall; this depends on your privacy settings as discussed in Chapter 3, Building Your Profile, starting on page 27.

For example, Stella can log in to Facebook and find Jim's Facebook pages using the search bar. Since Jim's privacy settings allow his posts to be viewed by Everyone, Stella can see Jim's photos, even though she is not one of Jim's Facebook friends. In the example below, in the top right-hand corner, you can see that it is **Stella** who is logged in on this computer. Having found Jim on Facebook using the search bar, the postings and photographs on his Wall are fully visible to Stella.

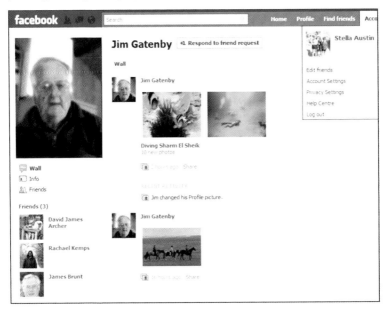

Any photographs which you don't want people who are not your friends to see should be set as **Friends only**, as described previously.

Uploading a Photo from Your Computer

Photographs stored on your computer's hard disc can easily be uploaded to the Facebook Web site. Photographs can also be uploaded from a removable medium such as a CD, DVD or flash drive (also known as a memory stick). Photographs can easily be transferred from a digital camera to your hard disc prior to uploading to Facebook. Old photographic prints may be scanned and saved on the hard disc. (These methods of transferring photographs to your computer are discussed in Chapter 8, Copying Photographs to Your Computer).

To upload a photograph already stored on your computer, from your Home page click **Photo** under **News Feed** as shown below or similarly from your Wall.

Now click **Upload a Photo** as shown above and then click the **Browse...** button. A window opens up allowing you to start searching the folders on your hard disc for the required image. Select the required file and click **Open**.

In the example below, an image named **beach riding.jpg** was selected from the folder called **Jills photos** on the hard disc drive, known as the **C:** drive on most computers.

Uploading a Photo from a Flash Drive

If you have a photograph saved on a removable storage device such as a flash drive or memory stick, the device will appear as something like **Removable Disk (E:)**, for example, as shown below. Similarly a CD/DVD drive usually appears as drive **(D:)**.

In the example above, the required photo image is called **Adult barn owl.JPG**, saved in a folder called **Wildlife** on the flash drive designated **Removable Disk (E:)**. When you click the **Open** button shown above, the full path name of the image appears as shown below.

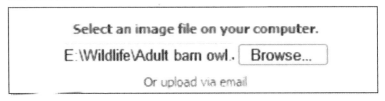

Sharing the Photograph

Having selected the required photograph, set the privacy such as **Friends only** using the menu opened by clicking the padlock icon shown on the right and at the bottom right below. Then click the **Share** button.

The photo quickly appears as an update on your Wall and on your Home page under News Feed.

The photo will also appear on the News Feed of people who are your Facebook friends. If the privacy is set to Everyone, people who are not your friends will be able to find you on Facebook using the search bar and then view the photograph on your Wall.

Enlarging a Photo Posted on the Wall

Clicking the small thumbnail image of the owl shown on the previous page displays the enlarged photo shown below.

Facebook Photo Albums

Photographs which you upload to Facebook from your hard disc or other storage device are automatically saved in an album called **Wall Photos** created by Facebook. On the next page the creation of your own photo albums is discussed. This method is used when you are uploading a large number of photographs.

The JPEG Photographic File Format

You may have noticed the letters **.jpg** or **.JPG** at the end of the names of photographic files as on page 77. The **.jpg** file name extension is short for Joint Photographic Experts Group. This is very common file format used for photographic files saved on digital cameras, computers and on the Internet.

Creating Photograph Albums

From your Home or Profile page, select **Photo** and click **Create an Album**, as shown below.

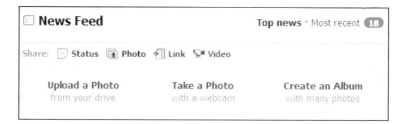

The **Upload photos** window opens from which you should click **Select photos**.

This opens the **Select file(s)...** window shown on the next page. Use this to browse your computer for the required photographs. As mentioned earlier, the photos may be in a folder on your hard disc, on a CD or DVD, or on a flash drive, for example.

To select multiple photos, click each photograph's file name while continuing to hold down the **Ctrl** key. This highlights the selected files in blue as shown on the next page.

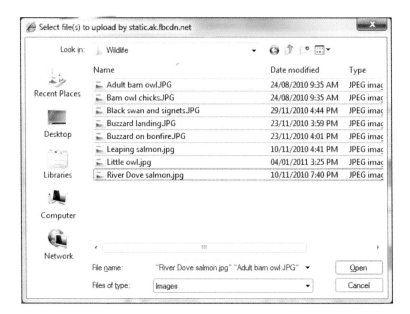

If you need to browse another device such as a CD/DVD or flash drive, click on the **Computer** icon shown above to display the other devices. When you click **Open** shown above, the **Upload photo** process begins in its own window, as shown below.

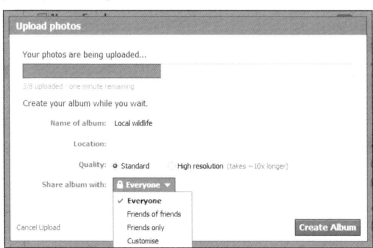

As shown on the previous page, while the photos are being uploaded you can give a name to the photo album. You can set the resolution to **Standard** or **High resolution**; standard will probably be quite satisfactory to display your photographs and will upload more quickly. You can also set the privacy to **Everyone**, **Friends only**, etc., while the photos are being uploaded.

When you have entered the details of the album click **Create Album**, as shown at the bottom of the previous page. The following window opens confirming that the upload is complete.

As shown above, you can either publish the photos to Facebook now or edit the photos, tag them and add comments before publishing. You can always tag and edit the photos later if you wish and these topics are discussed shortly.

If you click **Publish Now**, the album, **Local Wildlife** in this example, immediately opens as shown on the next page.

Nature Note: Wildlife enthusiasts might be interested to know that the migratory salmon shown in the picture on the next page were reintroduced into the River Dover in recent years by the Environment Agency and the Trent Rivers Trust. The buzzards shown on the bonfire are now a very common sight in parts of Derbyshire.

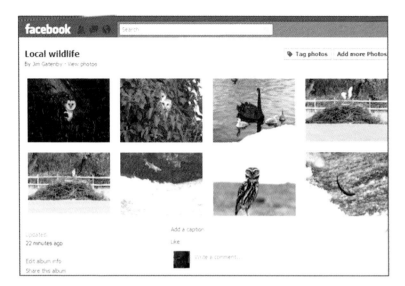

Click on a thumbnail to enlarge the photo as shown below.

Viewing Your Photo Albums

Sign in to Facebook then select **Profile** and click **Photos** from the small menu on the left-hand side.

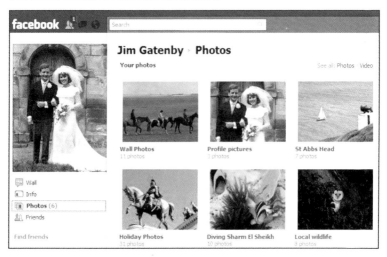

The **Profile pictures** album shown above is created automatically when you upload a profile picture. Similarly the **Wall Photos** album is created automatically when you upload single pictures from a webcam or from your hard disc, etc. The other albums shown above were all created as described on the previous pages. As mentioned earlier, each album can have up to 200 images and you can have as many albums as you like.

Editing a Photograph

Click on an album to display all the pictures within it, such as the album named **Diving Sharm El Sheikh**, which contains 10 photographs. Then click an individual photograph. The image opens filling most of the screen, as shown on the next page. At the bottom of the screen, there are spaces to add a caption for the image and to write a comment.

Clicking the album name on the small menu shown on the bottom right above returns you to the album. There are two icons to rotate the image and the **Share** option allows you to set privacy on the photo, such as **Friends only**, **Everyone**, etc. You can set the image as a profile picture to be used to identify you on Facebook and there is an option to delete the image.

A further option allows you to tag the photograph and this topic is discussed on the next page.

Tagging Photographs

If you have a photograph on Facebook which shows a group of people, tagging helps you to share the image with the people involved. When you tag a person in a photograph a connection is made with their Wall and they receive a notification saying that they have been tagged, including a copy of the photo. Anyone viewing a tagged photograph can pass their cursor over the people in the picture and see their names. In the example below a photograph from a family celebration was uploaded to Facebook from my hard disc drive as previously described.

Click **Tag this Photo** from the menu at the bottom right of the screen, as shown on the previous page. The cursor changes to a small cross-hair; move this over the first person and click the left mouse button. The menu shown on the previous page appears.

If the person's name is listed on the menu, click the adjacent check box. Otherwise type their name into the blank bar at the top. A space appears for you to enter their e-mail address. Even if they are not on Facebook they will still be tagged on the picture and will be e-mailed a copy of the picture. Click the **Tag** button shown on the previous page and repeat the process for the other people in the picture. Then click **Finished tagging** or **Done tagging** at the top right of the screen.

Any of your friends tagged in the picture will receive a notification that they have been tagged on their Wall, together with a thumbnail of the photo. Clicking this displays the full size photo; when they pass the cursor over each person in the photograph, the person's name appears as shown below. In a large gathering this makes it easy for people to share photographs and also view the names of other people in the photo. At the bottom of the picture the people tagged in the picture are listed and you can click an option to remove the tag or add a comment.

Photographs You Are Tagged In

With the latest version of Facebook, five photographs appear in a strip near the top, as shown below. These are a selection from the photos you are tagged in. You don't actually have to appear in the picture, just tag your name somewhere in the image, as described on pages 86 and 87.

As shown above, the strip of photos at the top of the Wall can include a favourite pet or car, for example. The photos in which your name is tagged also appear in **Photos and videos of you** shown below, displayed by clicking **Photos** off the **Profile** menu.

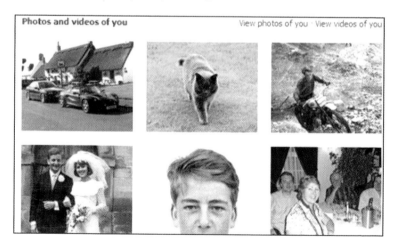

Putting Videos on Facebook Using a Webcam

You can share videos with friends on Facebook. From your Home Page or Wall, click **Video** as shown below. You can record your own video using a webcam or upload a video which has been saved on your hard disc drive as discussed shortly.

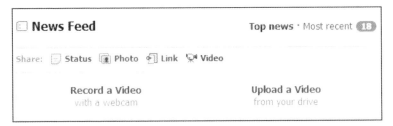

Recording a Video With a Webcam

For this option you need to have a webcam fitted to your computer. As discussed earlier, many new laptops have a built-in webcam or you can buy a separate webcam on a cable that can be moved or clipped to your computer monitor. In order to watch videos you also need a piece of software called Adobe Flash Player installed. This is known as a *plugin* and works with a Web browser such as Internet Explorer or Mozilla Firefox. Adobe Flash Player can be freely downloaded from **www.adobe.com**.

If you have a separate webcam, make sure it's connected. Click **Record a Video** shown above, then click the small round radio button next to **Allow** and click **Close,** as shown on the right. The video screen opens as shown on the next page. Initially  there is a red and white button to start the recording. After you start recording this changes to the stop button, shown here on the right.

After you click the stop button, the video window displays **Play** and **Reset** buttons and you can enter a note in the box to replace the words **Say something about this video...** as shown below.

Click the small padlock icon shown near the bottom right above and set the privacy level for the video to one of **Friends only**, **Friends of friends, Everyone** or **Customise**. The **Customise** setting allows you to make the video viewable by, or hidden from, specified people.

Finally click the **Share** button shown above to post the video to your friends' News Feeds.

Notification of a Video on a Friend's Wall

Your friend receives a notification of a video in their News Feeds and can click the white and blue play button shown above to start the video. The video is played in an enlarged window and can also be displayed full screen by clicking the button shown on the extreme right below.

As shown above, there are buttons to pause the video and also adjust the volume. The video is also posted on your own Wall and News Feed, enabling you to play it as described above.

Uploading Videos from Your Hard Disc

This section describes the copying of a video which had previously been saved on your computer's hard disc drive. Transferring a photo or video to the Facebook Website on the Internet in this way is generally known as Uploading.

The Windows Video Library

If you have Windows 7 you can easily practise this task using the sample videos stored in the video library. Click the Explorer icon on the Taskbar at the bottom of the screen, shown on the right and below.

Select **Libraries** from the left-hand side of the Explorer screen and then double-click the **Videos** icon as shown below.

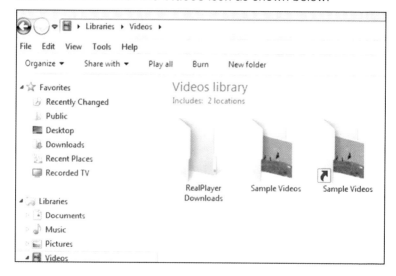

Double-click the **Sample Videos** folder shown above to see the icons for the stored videos such as the **Wildlife.wmv** video shown on the right.

Wildlife.wmv

Uploading a Video to Facebook

Now we know where the sample video is located on the hard disc drive, it's a simple job to upload it to Facebook. From your Home page select **Video** and **Upload a Video** as shown on page 89.

Now click **Browse...** and locate the sample video in the appropriate folder as shown on the previous page. The video is called **Wildlife.wmv** and is stored in the **Sample Videos** folder in the **Videos Library**. Click the video file name and then click **Open** to place the full path name of the video on the left of **Browse...** shown below.

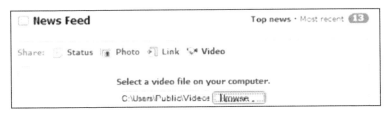

Now select the privacy level after clicking the small padlock icon, as shown on the right.

Click **Share** to start the process of uploading the file to Facebook. Please note there is a limit of 100MB or 2 minutes on the size of a video to be uploaded. As before, a notification including a thumbnail for the video appears on your Wall and on your News Feed and your friends' News Feeds. Click the small Play button shown on the right and below to watch the video in an enlarged window or full screen.

Key Facts: Facebook Photographs

- Photographs and videos are a major part of Facebook; as part of your personal profile a photo allows people who know you to recognise your pages on Facebook.

- Facebook enables millions of people to share their latest photos and videos with friends around the world.

- Facebook simplifies the process of uploading photos and videos from your computer to the Facebook Web site.

- Photographs can be uploaded from your hard disc drive or other storage medium such as a CD or DVD.

- You can use a webcam to take a photograph and upload it directly to Facebook.

- Share settings allow you to control who can see a photograph.

- Your recent photographs appear on your Wall and on your friends' Home page under News Feed.

- If the Share settings are set to Everyone, anyone who is not your friend might find you by searching on Facebook. They can then view your photographs and personal information on your Wall.

- Photos can be organised into albums, each album containing up to 200 photographs.

- People appearing in a photograph can be tagged with their name. This provides a link to the person's Wall with a notification that they have been tagged and including a thumbnail of the photograph.

- Clicking a thumbnail displays an enlarged image; passing the cursor over a tagged photograph displays the names of any people who have been tagged.

- Short videos can be uploaded and viewed on Facebook in a similar way to still photographs.

More Facebook Features

Introduction

Previous chapters have covered the basic skills needed to get started with Facebook and how to use the main features. These include your Profile, the Wall, News Feed, Facebook Friends, and involve communication in various forms such as status updates, photos, videos and links to Web sites, for example.

With these basic skills you should now be able to explore many other important features on Facebook such as those listed below and briefly described in the rest of this chapter.

- Facebook Mobile: Viewing your Facebook pages while on the move using a mobile phone.

- Apps: Software for various applications such as utilities for uploading photos and games and entertainment.

- Groups: Getting together online with other people to share information about a common interest.

- Notifications: Notes generated by Facebook informing you that something has happened on Facebook involving you.

- Networks: Facebook encompasses many networks based on schools, colleges and places of work. To join a network you need a valid e-mail address for the network.

- Events: Publicising forthcoming events with the place, date and time.

- Facebook Pages: special pages designed to promote a business, organisation, celebrity, cause or community.

Facebook on the Move

You can access Facebook from a mobile phone. With the latest Smartphones such as the iPhone or Blackberry (shown on the right) you can download a free Facebook App. This allows you to use miniature versions of most of the Facebook features available on a full-blown computer. With a phone of a lower specification than a Smartphone you may still be able to use some Facebook features. The number of features you can use depends on the specification of your phone, as follows.

- If your phone can use SMS (Short Message Service) you can send and receive short text messages between Facebook and your mobile phone. These can be used to update your status or receive notifications.

- A mobile phone that can use MMS (Multi-media Message Service) can be used to upload photos and videos to Facebook.

- If your phone has a Web browser you can access the Facebook Mobile Web site at **http://m.facebook.com**, where you can use most of the Facebook features such as status updates, Wall posts, News Feed and photos.

For help on setting up a mobile phone for Facebook, from the bottom right of your Home/ News Feed page click **Try Facebook mobile**. Alternatively from any of your Facebook pages, click **Account**, **Help Centre** and **Mobile**. You can also activate a mobile phone to receive Facebook text messages after clicking **Account**, **Account Settings** and **Mobile**. These include notifications, messages, Wall posts and status updates.

Facebook Apps

These are applications or programs which work within the Facebook environment. Some Apps are provided by Facebook itself such as the Events and Photos features while others, such as games, are produced by third-party developers.

Click **Apps** from the left-hand side of the Facebook Home page and then click **Apps Directory** under **Apps** on the top left of the centre panel. As shown below, there are many screens full of Apps, with various categories listed down the left-hand side.

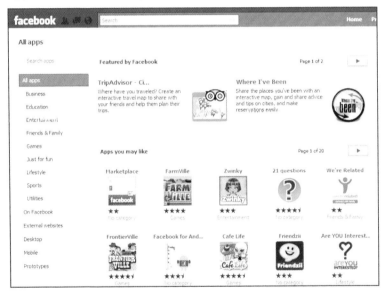

One of the most popular Apps is the game called Farmville. This is a real-time simulation of farms, played by Facebook members or "neighbours" who can work together on joint farming activities. Starting off with an empty farm, neighbours grow crops and raise animals to earn as much money as possible. Before using a particular App you can choose either to allow the App to access your personal information or click a button to leave the App.

Facebook Groups

A group on Facebook is a page shared by a number of people with a common interest. You can join a group you're interested in or create a new group of your own. A group can have just a few members or several thousand.

For example, you might want to find out about any groups already up and running on a particular subject, such as antiques. Enter **antiques** in the Facebook search bar and at the bottom of the first short list of results, click **See more results for antiques**.

A longer list of results appears from which you now click **Groups** on the left-hand side of the screen, as shown below.

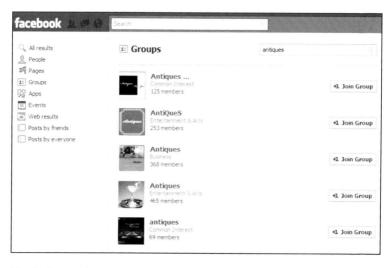

To find out about a group, click on its thumbnail photograph as shown above. The Facebook page for the group opens as shown on the next page. This is similar in format to your own Facebook page, with a Wall and Info sections as well as Discussions, Photos and Events. As shown on the **Info** page, anyone is welcome to join this particular group to share ideas, events, ask questions and talk about antiques. If you are interested click **Join Group** shown above or the **Join** button shown on the next page.

Creating Your Own Group

From the left-hand side of your Home page click **Create group** as shown on the next page. After a few seconds the **Create group** window opens as shown below.

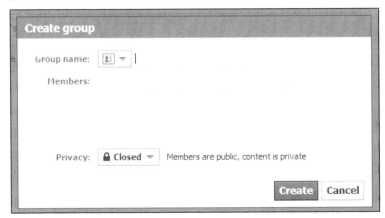

Enter a name for your group and select the privacy level from a drop-down menu with **Open**, **Closed** and **Secret** settings. Type in the names of the members of Facebook to invite to join the group. If they are friends of yours their names will pop up on a list and you can select them. Now click the **Create** button and the group is created and its name listed on the left-hand side of your Home page. As with a personal Profile, you can add a picture and a description for a group. The group can be edited at any time after clicking the group name and then **Edit Group**.

Notifications

These are messages from Facebook, informing you of activity on Facebook that involves you. You can check your notifications by clicking the third blue icon from the left on the blue bar, next to the word **facebook**, as shown on the right and below. A small red square appears on the blue bar, informing you of the number of new notifications.

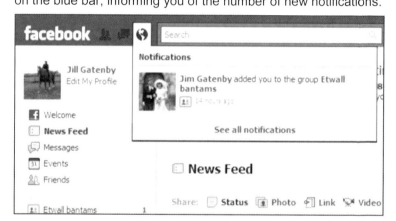

Networks

To access a local area network supported by Facebook, you must have a valid e-mail address provided by the school, college or company, etc. To join a network, click **Account**, from the right-hand side of the blue Facebook bar shown below. Then select **Account Settings** and **Networks** and enter the name of the network, your e-mail address and any other details required. Finally click the blue **Join Network** button shown below.

Events

This feature allows you to publicise the details of any future gathering you are planning and to send out invitations. Shown below is an extract from the Events section of the Facebook page belonging to the findmypast.co.uk Web site.

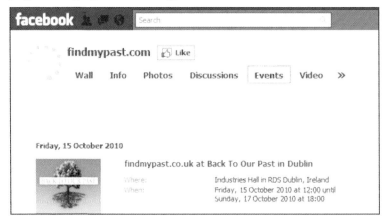

To create an event, from the left-hand side of your Home page click **Events** and then click **Create an event** from the top right. In the window shown below, enter the date, time, place and description of the event and click **Select guests** to invite friends. The tick boxes allow you to make the event public (anyone can view) or private (by invitation only). Then click **Create event**.

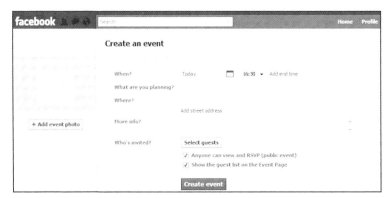

Pages for Businesses and Celebrities, etc.

You can set up a special Facebook Page to promote a business, cause, or celebrity, for example. On the initial Facebook Sign Up page, click **Create a Page for a celebrity, band or business**.

As shown below, you can create a Community Page for a cause or an Official Page for a business, product, artist, celebrity or public figure. To create an Official Page for a band, public figure, business or product, etc., click the small tick box at the lower right to confirm that you are their official representative. Then click the appropriate **Create** button as shown below.

You now start building your Page by uploading pictures, inserting notes and information, advertisements, links to Web sites and invitations for people to participate in the page. These Facebook Pages are similar to ordinary personal pages with a Wall, Photos, Info sections and updates but with the emphasis on promotion for a person or business or for gathering support for a cause.

8

Copying Photographs to Your Computer

Introduction

Earlier chapters have shown that photographs play a major part in the Facebook social network. Chapter 6 showed how photos which had been previously stored on your computer's hard disc drive could be uploaded to your Wall on the Facebook Web site. Then they can be shared by your friends and family. If you don't know how to copy photographs to your hard disc drive ready for uploading to Facebook, this chapter shows you how to:

- Copy recent photos from a digital camera and store them on your computer's hard disc drive.

- Scan an existing photographic print on glossy paper and save the image on the hard disc drive.

Digital Cameras

There are two main types of digital camera, the Compact and the Digital SLR (Single Lens Reflex). A compact digital camera is shown on the next page and is a general purpose camera capable of producing good quality photographs. Compact cameras typically cost from £60-£200; the digital SLR is favoured by enthusiasts and professionals, with prices starting around £350. The SLR camera is physically bigger than the pocket-sized compact and can be fitted with alternative lenses for different purposes, e.g. photographing far-away subjects or fast moving objects. Additional SLR lenses can be bought for around £100.

103

Memory Cards

Unlike their predecessor, the 35mm film camera, digital cameras store images on small removable memory cards, as shown on the right. Currently a 16GB (gigabyte) card capable of storing thousands of photographs is available for £13.99. Images stored on a  memory card can be copied to your computer's hard disc in various ways, as discussed shortly; old images can be deleted from the memory card and replaced by new images during your next photo session. You can repeat this process indefinitely.

Connecting a Camera to a Computer

The digital camera can be connected to one of the USB ports on the computer using a cable, usually provided with the camera, as shown below. The USB ports are small rectangular slots on the front or back of a desktop computer or on the side of a laptop.

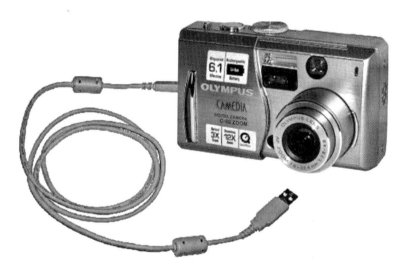

A Compact Digital Camera and USB Cable

Using a Separate Card Reader

The memory card can be connected to a computer using a separate memory card reader, as shown on the right. These only cost a few pounds and have a range of slots to accommodate different types of memory card such as SD, XD and CF. As shown on the right, a cable is

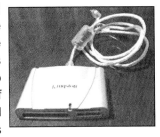

provided to connect the card reader to a USB port on the computer.

Memory Card Slots on a Printer

Many modern printers also have slots in which to insert various types of memory card. Typical card slots are shown below on the front of a Brother inkjet printer, at the top left-hand side.

It's a simple task to remove a memory card from a digital camera after opening a small spring-loaded cover. Then the card should be carefully inserted into the appropriate slot in the card reader or printer. There are several advantages to connecting devices such as cameras and card readers to the computer via the USB (Universal Serial Bus) ports shown on the previous page. For example, peripheral devices can be "hot swapped", i.e. connected while the computer is up and running, without the need to shut down and "reboot" the computer.

The Copying Process

With your computer up and running, connect the camera or card reader to the computer via one of the vacant USB ports. The camera should be switched on, as should the printer if you are using one to accommodate the memory card.

The memory card is detected by the Windows operating system and the **Autoplay** window appears, as shown below. In this example a camera is designated as **Removable Disk (G:)** but a different computer system might use **(E:)** or **(F:)** for example, depending on what other devices are connected. (When connected to the computer, the memory card can be treated like another disc drive; you can read from it or write data on it.)

Select **Import pictures and videos using Windows Live Photo Gallery**. As shown on the next page, you can either tick the **Select all** box to import all the photographs or just tick certain ones.

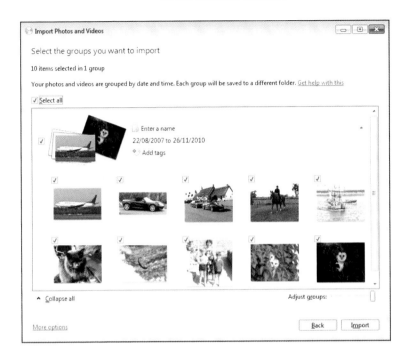

The pictures are automatically inserted into the Windows **Pictures library** in the Windows Explorer, as shown below.

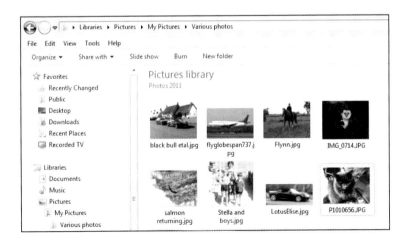

The Path to Your Photos

As described on the previous page, the photographs are imported from the memory card and automatically placed in the **Pictures** library, a location on the hard disc. As shown below and on the previous page, the path name specifies the exact location of the photos on the hard disc within a hierarchy of folders.

Libraries, **Pictures** and **My Pictures** are locations created on the hard disc drive when the Windows operating system was first installed. **Various photos** was a name I made up for the particular set of photos being imported. To view the folders at any time click the Windows Explorer icon on the Taskbar at the bottom of the screen.

Depending on the Folder Settings on your computer, click or double-click a folder to display the files in the folder. (You can set this in the Windows Explorer after selecting **Tools** and **Folder Options...**)

It's essential that you know the location of the folder on the hard disc drive containing your photographs. As discussed in Chapter 6, in order to upload the photos to the Facebook Web site, you must first browse to find the required folder. After selecting the required folder and file name for a photo on your hard disc, click **Open** to insert the path name next to **Browse..** shown below.

When you click **Share** the photo is uploaded to Facebook.

Copying Photos to Your Own Folders

As stated previously, Libraries, Pictures and My Pictures are used to automatically store the photographs you have imported to the computer from a camera or memory card reader, etc. In fact it's not difficult to create your own hierarchy of folders on the hard disc drive and copy your photographs to them.

Viewing the Memory Card Images on the Screen

Connect the camera, etc., to the computer and from the **Autoplay** window which appears click **Open folder to view files using Windows Explorer**. The Explorer window opens displaying the folders on your memory card. You may have to browse down through a hierarchy of folders. The path name to my photos is shown across the top of the window below. **Computer** is the name given to all of the storage devices on the computer system. **Removable Disk (G)** is the memory card, inserted in a card reader in this example. **DCIM** and **101-PANA** are default names of folders on the Panasonic Lumix camera.

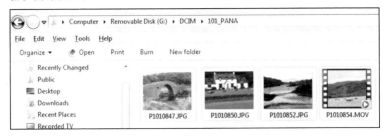

Creating a Hierarchy of New Folders

To create a new folder at the highest level on a hard disc drive, click the drive letter of the hard disc, usually **(C:)**. Then click **New folder** on the Explorer menu bar shown above and type the name of the new folder in the box, before pressing **Enter**.

To create a new sub-folder within an existing folder, select that folder with a single click. Then click **New folder**, type the name of the sub-folder in the box and press **Enter**. Sub-folders can be "nested" within sub-folders on several levels.

Selecting the Photos to be Copied

Now select the folder on the memory card **Removable Disk (G:)** as shown on the previous page and select all the photos you want to copy. To select multiple photos continue to hold down the **Ctrl** key while clicking each image in turn. When selected the photos should all be highlighted against a blue background.

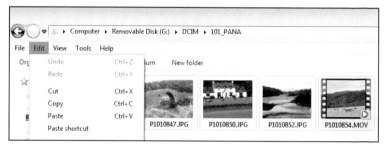

Copy and Paste

From the Explorer menu bar select **Edit** and **Copy** as shown above. The photographs are now placed on the Windows "clipboard". The clipboard is a temporary storage area where you can hold files and data before saving them to a new location.

Now that the photos have been copied to the clipboard they can be "pasted" into a folder on the hard disc. Select the new folder on the hard disc by clicking its name. Then from the **Edit** menu select **Paste**. This will copy the photos into the new folder on the hard disc. The above procedure is often referred to as "Copy and Paste" and is similar to "Cut and Paste". Unlike copy and paste, cut and paste deletes selected files from their original location.

As described above, the **Copy**, **Cut** and **Paste** operations all appear on the Explorer **Edit** menu. These options can also be selected after right-clicking over a file name or icon (such as one of the photo icons shown above). In the example on the next page, a folder called **Jims Photos** was created on the **(C:)** drive and a sub-folder, **Scotland**, created within, using the method just described.

Viewing and Editing Photographs

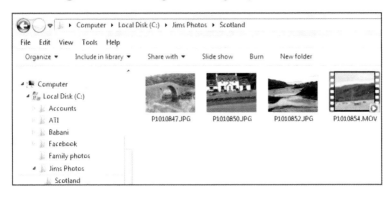

The images shown on the hard disc drive above were copied straight from a memory card to the clipboard of the computer. Then the sub-folder **Scotland** was selected and the **Paste** option selected from the **Edit** menu. The three images on the left are all in the **.JPG** format, widely used for photographs in computers and on the Internet. The image on the right is a video clip recorded on a compact digital camera. You can display the icons in different sizes by clicking **View** shown above and then selecting **Extra Large**, **Large**, **Medium** or **Small**.

If you double-click any of the icons, the photograph or video will open up in its associated program. Photos might open in the Windows Live Photo Gallery for example, while the video clip might open in the Windows Media Player. Alternatively right-click any of the icons and select **Open with** from the menu which appears. From the list of programs which appears choose the program you wish to use. For example, to crop, edit or enhance a photograph, you might select **Adobe Photoshop Elements**, **Microsoft Office Picture Manager**, or **Paint** as shown below.

Scanning a Photographic Print

You might want to share some of your existing photographic prints with friends and family who are users of Facebook. As previously described, uploading to Facebook is a simple matter if the images are already saved on your hard disc. In order to copy a paper print onto your hard disc drive, the photograph needs to be scanned and converted to a digital image. Multi-function printers containing a built-in scanner and the necessary software are available for under £50. Alternatively you can buy a separate flatbed scanner for a similar price. In the example below, a print is being scanned using the SmarThru software in a Samsung multi-function laser printer. The scanned image can be sent to various destinations such as the Paint program (i.e. application), or a folder on your hard disc or an e-mail message.

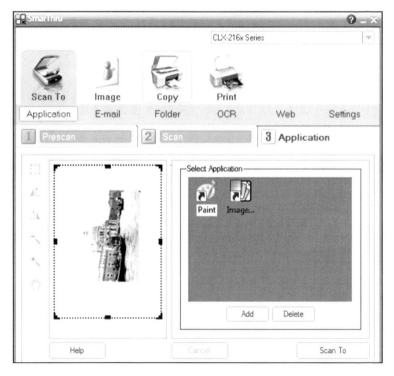

Editing an Image in Microsoft Paint

As shown on the previous page, the scanned image can be sent to the Microsoft Paint program. Paint is provided as part of the Windows operating system and can be opened by clicking **Start**, **All Programs**, **Accessories** and **Paint**.

Paint is basically a drawing program but there are various tools which can be used to edit a photograph such as resizing, cropping, rotating and adding a text caption. Use **Save as** to save the image in a folder on your hard disc in the JPEG or **.jpg** file format as shown below. Then it will be ready for uploading to Facebook as described in Chapter 6.

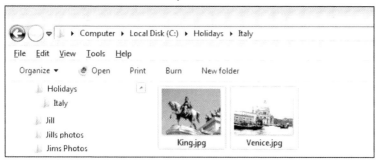

Archiving Photographs to a CD or DVD

Facebook has an option to upload photographs to the Web site from your hard disc, as discussed in Chapter 6. In fact, you can connect your camera or card reader to your computer and upload them directly to Facebook without saving them on your hard disc drive at all. While this would be alright if you want to give your friends a quick look at a few photos, it would not be a good idea for a large number of photographs. You would soon want to delete the photographs from the memory card in the camera to make room for new ones, leaving only the copies on Facebook.

Copying photos to your hard disc drive as previously described would give you some fairly secure copies. Copies on the hard disc can easily be enhanced, edited, cropped and uploaded to Facebook. However, even photographs stored on the hard disc are not completely secure; the hard disc drive can be accidentally wiped or it may need to be reformatted (i.e. deliberately wiped) to overcome a software problem, causing all of the photos to be lost. Families have been known to lose entire collections of irreplaceable photographs because they didn't have a secure backup copy of their precious albums.

A good way to archive your photos securely is to copy them to a CD-R or DVD-R. These will store hundreds and thousands of photos respectively and can only be written to once. Unlike the CD-RW and DVD-RW you can't delete or write over the photos on a CD-R or DVD-R. You can back up your photos to a CD-R or DVD-R using the following method:

- Place a blank CD/DVD in the drive and format it.
- Select the required folder in the Windows Explorer.
- Right-click over the folder and click **Copy**.
- Select the CD/DVD drive in Explorer and click **Paste**.
- Click **Burn** to copy the photographs to the CD/DVD.
- Label the CD/DVD and keep it in a safe place.

A Glossary of Facebook Terms

Applications   Usually known as Apps for short, these are programs on Facebook such as games and software for uploading photographs.

Chat   This facility allows you to have a real-time conversation with friends by typing the words into a small window on the screen.

Comment   This enables you to type a short note in response to a status update or photograph.

Events   This feature allows you to inform friends about future events and social occasions.

Facebook   A worldwide social network with over 500 million members, exchanging news and information, photographs and videos.

Friend   A person whose invitation you've accepted to share information and news.

Friend request   An offer of friendship on Facebook which can be either accepted or declined

Group   This feature allows Facebook users to collaborate with other people sharing a common interest and to join online forums.

Home page   The Home page contains your News Feed and links to many other features such as Messages, Events and Friends.

Like   Clicking the word **Like** is a quick way to register your approval of an update or photo.

Message   A note sent to a particular friend or friends, similar to an e-mail. May include photos, etc.

News Feed   Part of your Home page, informing you of your friends' latest activities on Facebook.

Notifications   These are short messages which pop up on the screen telling you about something that happened on Facebook.

Page   Page in this context refers to a special feature for businesses, organisations, bands and celebrities, etc., to broadcast information to a wide audience.

Poke   This is a way of saying hello to a friend and reminding them you exist.

Post   A status update, photo or video placed on your Wall or on a friend's Wall.

Privacy Settings   Settings which allow you to control who can share which parts of your Facebook information and photographs, etc.

Profile   Your profile lists your personal information, photos, career and interests as well as posts stating what you've been doing on Facebook.

Status   A short update to friends saying what you're doing or what's on your mind. A photo, video or Web link can be attached. Friends can reply by writing a comment or clicking **Like**.

Tagging   Labelling a friend's name on a photo, sending an update and the photo to the friend's Wall.

Wall   A page listing all your activity on Facebook; photos, status updates and posts from your friends. Posts to your Wall are known as mini-feeds.

Webcam   A small camera which plugs into a USB port on a computer or which is built into a laptop. Used to take profile photos or pictures of objects close to the computer.

Index